BAR AND
RESTAURANT LOGOS

Edited by
David E. Carter

Art Director
Suzanna M.W. Stephens

Book Designer
Karen Moseley

Jacket Designer
Graham Allen

BAR AND RESTAURANT LOGOS

First published in 2000 by HBI,
an imprint of HarperCollins Publishers
10 East 53rd Street
New York, NY 10022-5299

ISBN: 0688-17992-4

Distributed in the U.S. and Canada by
Watson-Guptill Publications
770 Broadway
New York, NY 10003-9595
Tel: (800) 451-1741
          (732) 363-4511 in NJ, AK, HI
Fax: (732) 363-0338

ISBN: 0-8230-7351-3

Distributed throughout the rest of the world by
HarperCollins International
10 East 53rd Street
New York, NY 10022-5299
Fax: (212) 207-7654

First published in Germany by Nippan
Nippon Shuppan Hanbai
Deutschland GmbH
Krefelder Strasse 85
D-40549 Dusseldorf
Tel: (0211) 5048089
Fax: (0211) 5049326
nippan@t-online.de

Printed in Hong Kong by Everbest Printing Company through
Four Colour Imports, Louisville, Kentucky.

I was sitting in this bar, or maybe it was a restaurant with a bar. Whatever. I was watching the ice in my drink melt when I started sketching on the napkin. As jazz music played in the background, I wrote "Bar & Restaurant Logos Book" on the napkin—and that's how this book came to be.

Wait…that's not true. I made it up. Or maybe it was a scene I saw in an old film noir movie (except for the book title).

What actually happened was that I was sitting in my publisher's office in New York City (with not a drink in sight) when someone said "*Logos of American Restaurants* was a big seller. How about a follow-up book on bar and restaurant logos?"

I said "OK" and some months later, this book magically appeared. (I left out a lot of stuff here; in putting together a book like this, nothing happens fast and nothing happens magically*.)

Anyway, what you have here is a showcase of some of the best new logos (and their applications) for bars and restaurants. If you design logos for this market—or aspire to—this book has hundreds of great ideas which will spur your creativity to new heights.

Enjoy.

David. E. Carter

Creative Firm
Iridium Marketing & Design/Formerly Aartvark Comm.
Ottawa, Canada
Client
Las Palmas Mexican Restaurants
Designer
Jean-Luc Denat

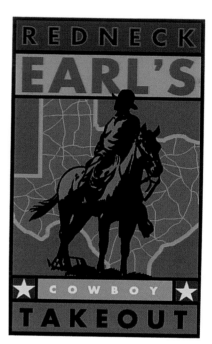

Creative Firm
Artefact Design
Palo Alto, California
Client
Redneck Earls Cowboy Takeout
Designer
Artefact Design

Creative Firm
Gardner Design
Wichita, Kansas
Client
Cactus Cuisine
Designer
Bill Gardner

Creative Firm
Gardner Design
Wichita, Kansas
Client
Fidel Bistro
Designer
Travis Brown

Creative Firm
Hornall Anderson Design Works
Seattle, Washington
Client
Casa de Ninos
Designers
Jack Anderson, David Bates

Creative Firm
Belyea
Seattle, Washington
Client
PCC Northwest Taste
Art Director
Patricia Belyea
Designer
Christian Salas

At PCC Natural Markets

Creative Firm
  Gottschalk+Ash International
  Zurich, Switzerland
Client
  Restaurant Freischütz
Designers
  Fritz Gottschalk, Regina Rodrigues

Creative Firm
  Di Vision Studio
  New York, New York
Client
  Rookies
Designers
  Carlo Pierallini, Joanne Lew, Cristiana Neri-Downey

Creative Firm
  Lang/Durham & Co.
  Meriden, Connecticut
Client
  Hilton-Hartford
Designer
  John M. Mik

Creative Firm
On Target
Los Angeles, California
Client
KWGB
Designers
Pam Patterson, Kathleen Livingston

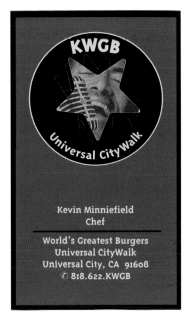

Creative Firm
David Carter Design Assoc.
Dallas, Texas
Client
Grand Hyatt Berlin
Designer
Ashley Barron

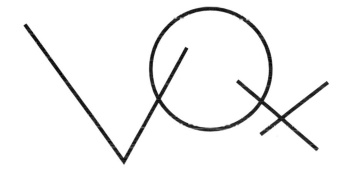

Creative Firm
William Ho Design Associates Ltd.
Hong Kong, China
Client
Patio Cafe, Tokyo, Japan
Designers
William Ho Chung Keung, Lam Wai Hung

Creative Firm
Diamant Design
New York, New York
Client
Payard Patisserie Bistro
Designer
Ellen Diamant

Payard

PATISSERIE & BISTRO

Creative Firm
Diamant Design
(continued)

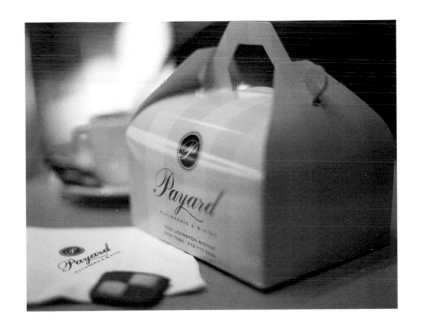

Creative Firm
   Vitro Robertson
   Carlsbad, California
Client
   Rubio's Baja Grill
Designers
   Jeff Payne, Tracy Sabin

Creative Firm
   Maddocks & Co.
   Carlsbad, California
Client
   El Cholo
Designers
   Clare Sebenius, Tracy Sabin

Creative Firm
   Vitro Robertson
   Carlsbad, California
Client
   Rubio's Baja Grill
Designers
   John Vitro, Tracy Sabin

Creative Firm
GSD&M
Austin, Texas
Client
Chili's Grill & Bar
Designer
Matt Mason

Creative Firm
GSD&M
Austin, Texas
Client
Chili's Grill & Bar
Designer
Matt Mason

Creative Firm
GSD&M
Austin, Texas
Client
Chili's Grill & Bar
Designer
Matt Mason
Illustrator
Paul Rogers

FATHOMS

Creative Firm
David Carter Design Assoc.
Dallas, Texas
Client
Atlantis Hotel, Paradise Island
Designer
Tien Pham

Creative Firm
David Carter Design Assoc.
Dallas, Texas
Client
Paradise Island
Designer
Ricky Brown

FIVE TWINS

Creative Firm
David Carter Design Assoc.
Dallas, Texas
Client
Atlantis Hotel, Paradise Island
Designer
Sharon LeJeune

Creative Firm
David Carter Design Assoc.
Dallas, Texas
Client
Paradise Island Resort & Casino
Designer
Gary LoBue

Creative Firm
David Carter Design Assoc.
Dallas, Texas
Client
Atlantis Hotel, Paradise Island
Designer
Kevin Prejean

Seagrapes

voyagers

PAPPAGALLO

Creative Firm
Allan Miller & Associates
El Cajon, California
Client
Pappagallo Pizza
Designer
Allan Miller

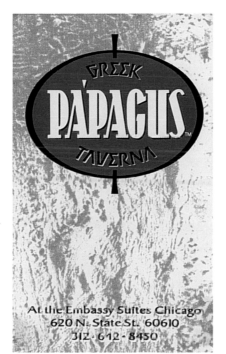

Creative Firm
True Ideas, Inc.
Chicago, Illinois
Client
Lettuce Entertain You Enterprises, Inc.
Designer
Cynthia Kerby, Ignatius Aloysius
Lettering Artist
Eliza Schulte

GREEK
PÁPAGUS™
TAVERNA

At the Embassy Suites Chicago
620 N. State St. 60610
312-612-8450

Creative Firm
Snodgrass Design Associates
Seattle, Washington
Client
Ruby's Restaurant
Designer
Leslie Snodgrass

Creative Firm
Cyd Design
   Milwaukee, Wisconsin
Client
   Zero Smoothies & Juice
   Bar
Designer
   Cory Dewalt

Creative Firm
Vrontikis Design Office
Los Angeles, California
Client
Global-Dining, Inc.
Designers
Tammy Kim, Petrula Vrontikis

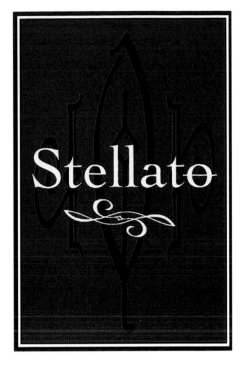

Creative Firm
Funk & Associates
Eugene, Oregon
Client
Marche Cafe
Designer
Beverly Soasey

Creative Firm
Richards & Swensen, Inc.
Salt Lake City, Utah
Client
ZCMI Center
Designer
Michael Richards

Creative Firm
Louey/Rubino Design Group, Inc.
Santa Monica, California
Client
Zen Palate (restaurant)
Designer
Robert Louey

Creative Firm
Vrontikis Design
New York, New York
Client
Cafe La Bohème
Designer
Lorna Stovall

Creative Firm
Funk and Associates
Eugene, Oregon
Client
Epping
Designer
Beverly Soasey

PARK 5

BISTRO

Creative Firm
Spencer Zahn & Associates
Philadelphia, Pennsylvania
Client
East Side Club
Designer
Spencer Zahn

VINTAGE

You are cordially invited to an event at

ViNTaGe

753 Ninth Avenue at 51st   New York, NY 10019
212·581·4624   212·581·4655

Bar   Restaurant   Catering

Creative Firm
Kelleher Design
New York, New York
Client
Vintage
Designers
Karen Kelleher, Douglas Tait

Creative Firm
  William Ho Design Associates Ltd.
  Hong Kong, China
Client
  Uncle Russ Cafe
  Hong Kong
Designer
  William Ho Chung Keung

Creative Firm
  Wynn Creative
  Soquel, California
Client
  Traveler's Pub & Cafe/Seattle
Designer
  Christopher Wynn

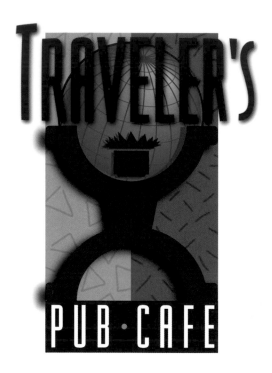

Creative Firm
  William Ho Design Associates Ltd.
  Hong Kong, China
Client
  Vimanloy Thai Cuisine
  Bangkok, Thailand
Designer
  William Ho Chung Keung

20

Creative Firm
  revoLUZion–Studio For Design
  Neuhausen ab Eck, Germany
Client
  ParcFerme, Karting Bar, Tommi Martin
Designer
  Bernd Luz

Creative Firm
  David Carter Design Assoc.
  Dallas, Texas
Client
  Dani
Designer
  Tracy Huck

Creative Firm
  Lieber Cooper Associates
  Chicago, Illinois
Client
  Taj Group of Hotels
  India
Designer
  Tobias Harris W.

Creative Firm
Hornall Anderson Design Works
Seattle, Washington
Client
Mondeo
Designers
Jack Anderson, David Bates, Sonja Max

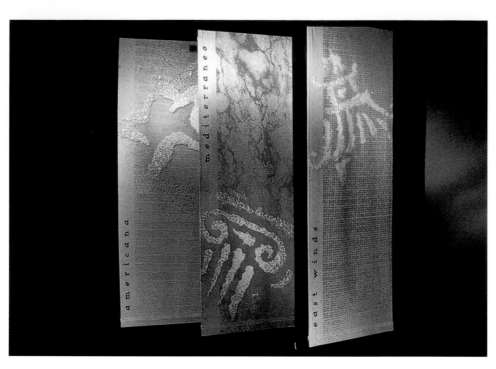

Creative Firm
Hornall Anderson Design Works
(continued)

Creative Firm
Hornall Anderson Design Works
(continued)

Creative Firm
aire design company
Tucson, Arizonia
Client
Small Planet Bakery
Designers
Steve Romaniello, Catharine M. Kim

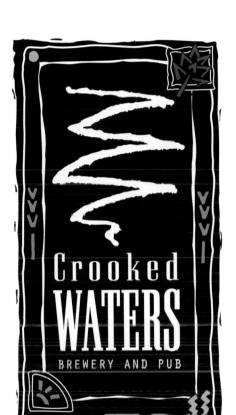

Creative Firm
Simantel Group
Peoria, Illinois
Client
Crooked Waters Brewery and Pub
Designers
Molly Vonachen, Wendy Behrens

Creative Firm
David Lemley Design
Seattle, Washington
Client
Pacific Bagel
Designer
David Lemley

Creative Firm
David Lemley Design
  Seattle, Washington
Client
  Starbucks Coffee
Designer
  David Lemley

Creative Firm
  David Lemley Design
  Seattle, Washington
Client
  Circadia Alla Fiama
Designer
  David Lemley

Creative Firm
  Ford & Earl Assoc.
  Troy, Michigan
Client
  Larco's
Designer
  Francheska Guerrero

LARCO's
ITALIAN CHOPHOUSE

Creative Firm
  David Lemley Design
  Seattle, Washington
Client
  CML Espresso
Designer
  David Lemley

Creative Firm
  Morla Design
    Seattle, Washington
Client
  Ristorante Ecco
Designers
  Jennifer Morla, Craig Bailey

Creative Firm
Tom Fowler, Inc.
Stamford, Connecticut
Client
Bar and Books
Designer
Thomas G. Fowler

Creative Firm
Little & Company
Minneapolis, Minnesota
Client
D'Amico & Sons, Metropolitan Logo
Creative Director
Monica Little
Design Director
Jim Jackson
Designer
Tom Riddle

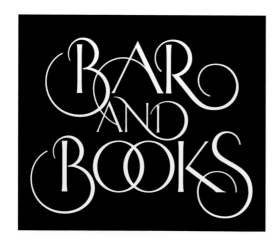

Creative Firm
Tom Fowler, Inc.
Stamford, Connecticut
Client
Bar and Books
Designer
Thomas G. Fowler

Creative Firm
IE Design
   Studio City, California
Client
   The Continental
Designers
   Cya Nelson, David Gilmour, Marcie Carson

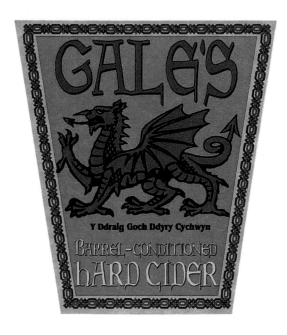

Creative Firm
The Thomas Family Winery (in-house)
Madison, Indiana
Client
Gale's Hard Cider
Designer
Steven L. Thomas

Creative Firm
Michael Niblett Design
Fort Worth, Texas
Client
The Argonaut Greek Restaurant
Designer
Michael Niblett

Creative Firm
Moby Dick Group
Szczecin, Poland
Client
"Unity Line"–Ferry Line
Designer
Wojciech Mierowski

Creative Firm
Brown Communications Group
Regina, Canada
Client
The Green Onion
Designer
Randy Hergott

CAMPAGNE

French Country Cuisine

Creative Firm
Kim Baer Design Associates
Venice, California
Client
Campagne Restaurant
Designer
Barbara Cooper

Creative Firm
revoLUZion–Studio For Design
Neuhausen ab Eck, Germany
Client
Bernhard Hansky, Landhaus Donautal
Designer
Bernd Luz

HOTEL · RESTAURANT

LANDHAUS DONAUTAL

BERGSTEIG

Creative Firm
Hornall Anderson Design Works
Seattle, Washington
Client
Best Cellars
Designers
Jack Anderson, Lisa Cerveny, Jana Wilson Esser,
Nicole Bloss, David Bates

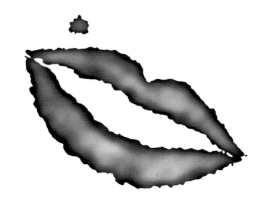

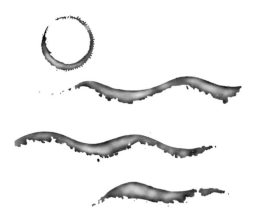

Creative Firm
Hornall Anderson Design Works.
(continued)

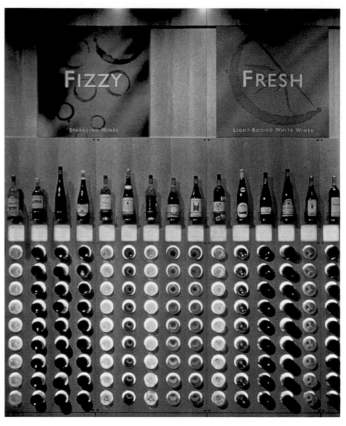

Creative Firm
  Phoenix Creative, St. Louis
  St. Louis, Missouri
Client
  Big Cat Enterprises
Designer
  Kathy Wilkinson

Creative Firm
  Creative Link Studio, Inc.
  Seattle, Washington
Client
  The Havana House–Club Cohiba
Designer
  Mark Broderick

Creative Firm
  Phoenix Creative, St. Louis
  St. Louis, Missouri
Client
  Big Cat Enterprises
Designer
  Kathy Wilkinson

Creative Firm
  Vrontikis Design Office
  Los Angeles, California
Client
  Global-Dining, Inc.
  Tokyo
Art Director
  Petrula Vrontikis
Designer
  Peggy Woo

Creative Firm
Pepe Gimeno–Proyecto Gráfico
   Godella, Spain
Client
   Huerto De Santa Maria
Designer
   Sebastián Alós

Creative Firm
McElveney & Palozzi Design Group, Inc.
Rochester, New York
Client
The Lodge at Woodcliff
Designer
Ellen Johnson

THE LODGE AT WOODCLIFF

Creative Firm
David Carter Design Assoc.
Dallas, Texas
Client
The Princeton Dubai
Designer
Gary LoBue

Creative Firm
The Thomas Family Winery (in-house)
Madison, Indiana
Client
The Thomas Family Winery
Designer
Steve L. Thomas

ROSTI
ROSTICCERIA TOSCANA

Creative Firm
Kim Baer Design Associates
Venice, California
Client
Rosti
Designer
Barbara Cooper

Creative Firm
David Carter Design Assoc.
Dallas, Texas
Client
Paris Resort & Casino
Las Vegas, NV
Designer
Ashley Barron

le café
île st. louis

Creative Firm
William Ho Design Associates Ltd.
Hong Kong, China
Client
The Continental, Tokyo, Japan
Designer
William Ho Chung Keung

THE
CONTINENTAL

Creative Firm
David Carter Design Assoc.
Dallas, Texas
Client
Paris Resort & Casino,
Las Vegas, NV
Designer
Kevin Prejean

Creative Firm
Hornall Anderson Design Works
Seattle, Washington
Client
Canal Place Cafe
Designer
Jack Anderson

Creative Firm
David Carter Design Assoc.
Dallas, Texas
Client
Paris Resort & Casino
Las Vegas, NV
Designer
Tabitha Bogard

Creative Firm
Rick Johnson & Co. Inc.
  Albuquerque, New Mexico
Client
  Doubletree Hotel
Designer
  Mark Chamberlain

Creative Firm
Kim Baer Design Associates
  Venice, California
Client
  Toscana
Designer
  Barbara Cooper

TOSCANA

Creative Firm
Callery & Company
  Patchogue, New York
Client
  Fine Baked Goods
Designer
  Kelley Callery

Creative Firm
Ritz Henton Design Group
Essex, Connecticut
Client
Pier Ponts

Creative Firm
Louey/Rubino Design Group, Inc.
Santa Monica, California
Client
Le Bar Bat (nightclub)
Designer
Robert Louey

Creative Firm
Adkins/Balchunas
Providence, Rhode Island
Client
Boston Restaurant Associates
Creative Director
Jerry Balchunas
Designer
Michelle Phaneuf

Creative Firm
Sayles Graphic Design
Des Moines, Iowa
Client
Colletti's Restaurant
Designer
John Sayles

THE
ARTICHOKE
CAFE

Creative Firm
Studio Hill Design
Albuquerque, New Mexico
Client
Artichoke Cafe
Designers
Sandy Hill, Emma Roberts

Creative Firm
Cisneros Design
Santa Fe, New Mexico
Client
Blue Corn Cafe
Designer
Fred Cisneros

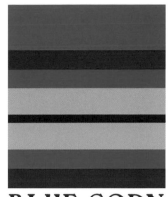

Creative Firm
Design Kitchen Inc.
Chicago, Illinois
Client
Cosentino's Restaurants
Designer
Jamie Anderson

Creative Firm
Louey/Rubino Design Group Inc.
Santa Monica, California
Client
Tutto Bene
Designer
Robert Louey

Creative Firm
  Girvin
  Seattle, Washington
Client
  Cascadia/Kerry Sean
Designers
  Tim Girvin, Jeff Haack, Kim Edberg,
  Michael Stearns, Valerie Degiulio,
  Damon Law

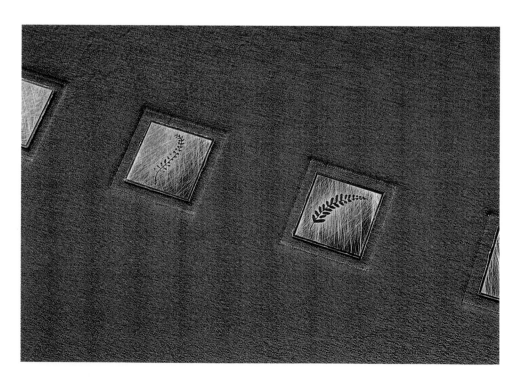

Creative Firm
JOED Design
Elmhurst, Illinois
Client
Pehrson Long
Designer
Edward Rebek

Creative Firm
Simantel Group
Peoria, Illinois
Client
Petticoats & Crumpets Tearoom
Designer
Randy Marx

Creative Firm
The Leonhardt Group
Seattle, Washington
Client
Andaluca
Designer
Renee Sullivan

ANDALUCA

Creative Firm
   King Casey, Inc.
   New Canaan, Connecticut
Client
   Sizzler
Designer
   John Chrzanowski

Creative Firm
   Yoe! Studio
   Peekskill, New York
Client
   Elias Brothers
Designer
   Yoe! Studio

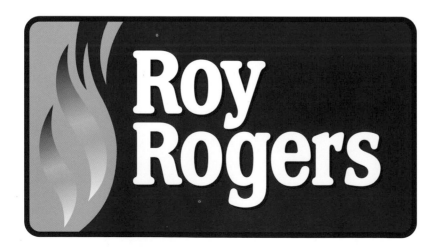

Creative Firm
   King Casey, Inc.
   New Cannan, Connecticut
Client
   Roy Rogers
Designers
   John Chrzanowski,
   Christen Kucharic

Creative Firm
King Casey, Inc.
New Canaan, Connecticut
Client
Denny's
Designer
John Chrzanowski

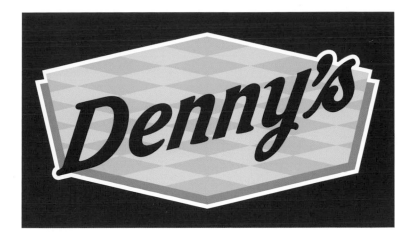

Creative Firm
King Casey, Inc.
New Canaan, Connecticut
Client
Denny's
Designer
John Chrzanowski

Creative Firm
Frankel & Company
St. Louis, Missouri
Client
McDonald's
Art Director
Scott Melton

Creative Firm
Grand Design Consultants Ltd.
Hong Kong, China
Client
Superbowl, Hong Kong
Designer
Grand So

Creative Firm
Di Vision Studio
New York, New York
Client
One 3 Restaurant Lounge
Designers
Cristiana Neri-Downey, Carlo Pierallini

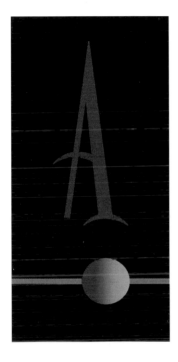

Creative Firm
David Carter Design Assoc.
Dallas, Texas
Client
Abacus Restaurant, Dallas, TX
Designer
Emily Cain

Creative Firm
Addison Design Consultants Pte Ltd
Singapore
Client
Shihlin Electric & Engineering Corporation
Designers
The Addison Creative Team

LOBBY LOUNGE

Creative Firm
Sayles Graphic Design
Des Moines, Iowa
Client
801 Steak & Chop House
Designer
John Sayles

Creative Firm
Sayles Graphic Design
(continued)

Creative Firm
Sayles Graphic Design
(continued)

Creative Firm
Sayles Graphic Design
(continued)

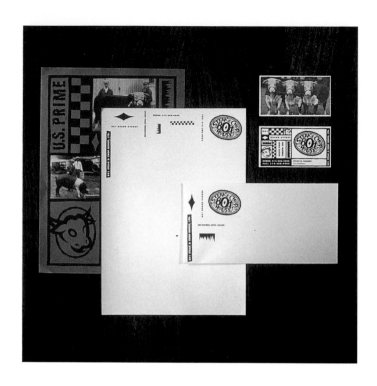

Creative Firm
Sayles Graphic Design
(continued)

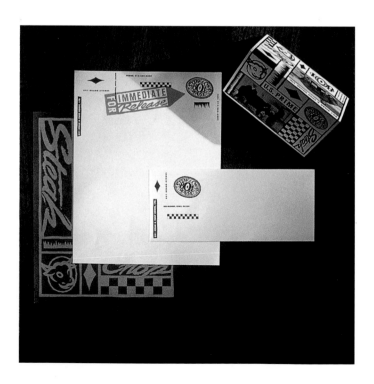

Creative Firm
RBMM
Dallas, Texas
Client
The Riviera
Designer
RBMM

Creative Firm
Muller + Company
Kansas City, Missouri
Client
The American Restaurant
Designers
John Muller, Joann Otto

Creative Firm
David Lemley Design
Seattle, Washington
Client
SLDU (2218 Club)
Designer
David Lemley

Creative Firm
Berry Design, Inc.
Alpharetta, Georgia
Client
Popeyes Chicken & Biscuits
Designer
Bob Berry

Creative Firm
Berry Design, Inc.
   Alpharetta, Georgia
Client
   Popeyes Chicken & Biscuits
Designer
   Bob Berry

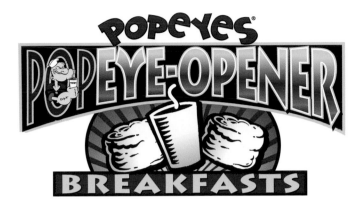

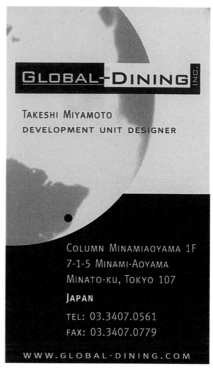

GLOBAL-DINING INC.

Creative Firm
Vrontikis Design Office
  Los Angeles, California
Client
  Global-Dining, Inc.
Designer/Art Director
  Petrula Vrontikis

TEL: 03.3407.0561
FAX: 03.3407.0779

WWW.GLOBAL-DINING.COM

〒107東京都港区南青山7-1-5
コラム南青山1F
株式会社 グローバルダイニング

COLUMN MINAMIAOYAMA 1F
7-1-5 MINAMI-AOYAMA
MINATO-KU, TOKYO 107
JAPAN

Creative Firm
Horvath Design
  Overland Park, Kansas
Client
  Steve Allen Design
Designer
  Kevin Horvath

Creative Firm
Heckler Associates
Client
  Associated Vitners
Designer
  Doug Fast

Silberkugel

Creative Firm
Lippincott & Margulies, Inc.
Client
  Movenpik
Designer
  Arthur Congdon

Creative Firm
Snodgrass Design Associates
Seattle, Washington
Client
Chez Shea Restaurant
Designer
Leslie Snodgrass

Creative Firm
Gardner Design
   Wichita, Kansas
Client
   Roosevelt's
Designer
   Travis Brown

明園西餐廳

MING GARDEN
International Cuisine

Creative Firm
Addison Design Consultants Pte Ltd
   Singapore
Client
   Shihlin Electric & Engineering Corporation
Designers
   The Addison Creative Team

Creative Firm
Boelts Bros. Assoc.
   Tucson, Arizona
Client
   The Manning House
Designers
   Jackson Boelts, Eric Boelts, Kerry Stratford

Creative Firm
CYD Design
  Milwaukee, Wisconsin
Client
  Vitucci's
Designer
  Cory Dewalt
Illustrator
  Jon Hargreaves

Creative Firm
Gardner Design
Wichita, Kansas
Client
Carlos O'Kellys
Designer
Chris Parks

Creative Firm
Icon Graphics, Inc.
Rochester, New York
Client
The Chicago Grill
Designer
Icon Graphics, Inc.

STEAK   PASTA

CHICAGO

GRILL

GLEN ALLEN

NORTH SHORE PRIME

Creative Firm
Beau Gardner Associates
New York, New York
Client
Glen Allen
Designer
Beau Gardner

Creative Firm
IE Design
Studio City, California
Client
Pete's
Designer
Marcie Carson

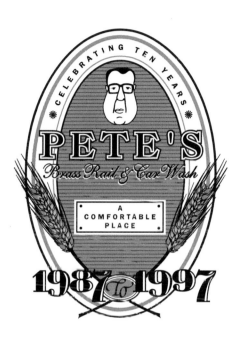

Creative Firm
David Carter Design Assoc.
Dallas, Texas
Client
Disney Cruise Line
Designers
Randall Hill, Cynthia Carter,
Lynn Pendergrass

Creative Firm
David Carter Design Assoc.
Dallas, Texas
Client
Disney Cruise Line
Designers
Cynthia Carter, Lynn Pendergrass

Creative Firm
David Carter Design Assoc.
Dallas, Texas
Client
Disney Cruise Line
Designer
Randall Hill

Creative Firm
David Carter Design Assoc.
Dallas, Texas
Client
Disney Cruise Line
Designer
Emily Cain

Creative Firm
David Carter Design Assoc.
Dallas, Texas
Client
Disney Cruise Line
Designer
Gary LoBue

Creative Firm
David Carter Design Assoc.
Dallas, Texas
Client
Disney Cruise Line
Designer
Tien Pham

Up bEaT

Creative Firm
David Carter Design Assoc.
Dallas, Texas
Client
Disney Cruise Line
Designer
Ricky Brown

Creative Firm
David Carter Design Assoc.
Dallas, Texas
Client
Disney Cruise Line
Designer
Tien Pham

Creative Firm
David Carter Design Assoc.
Dallas, Texas
Client
Disney Cruise Line
Designer
Ricky Brown

Creative Firm
David Carter Design Assoc.
Dallas, Texas
Client
Disney Cruise Line
Designer
Sharon LeJeune

Creative Firm
David Carter Design Assoc.
Dallas, Texas
Client
Disney Cruise Line
Designer
Paul Munsterman

Creative Firm
Sayles Graphic Design
Des Moines, Iowa
Client
Hungry Camper
Designer
John Sayles

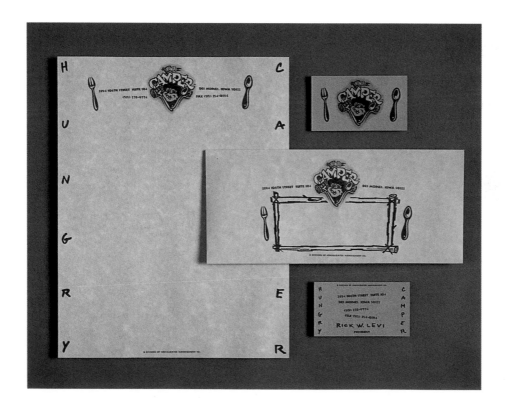

KARAOKE CLUB

Creative Firm
Addison Design Consultants Pte Ltd
Singapore
Client
Shihlin Electric & Engineering Corporation
Designers
The Addison Creative Team

Creative Firm
William Ho Design Associates Ltd.
Hong Kong, China
Client
The Bar
Bangkok, Thailand
Designer
William Ho Chung Keung

mont★d'or

KARAOKE LOUNGE

Creative Firm
Profile Design
San Francisco, California
Client
Hotel Kinzan
Arima, Japan
Designer
Profile Design

Creative Firm
Grand Design Consultants Ltd.
Hong Kong, China
Client
Yindo Hotel (Shanghai Restaurant)
Designer
Grand So

Three Arrows Chinese Restaurant

Creative Firm
Ammirati Puris Lintas
Singapore
Client
Three Arrows Chinese Restaurant
Designer
Vancelee Teng

Creative Firm
Addison Design Consultants Pte Ltd
Singapore
Client
Shihlin Electric & Engineering Corporation
Designers
The Addison Creative Team

CANTON COURT

粵菜廳

SUSHI SAKE

Creative Firm
David Carter Design Assoc.
Dallas, Texas
Designer
Tien Pham

Creative Firm
Fusion Art Institute
Susono-shi, Japan
Client
Cafe Keyaki
Designers
Hyomon, Fumihiko Enokido,
Hideaki Enokido

Creative Firm
Bruce Yelaska Design
   San Francisco, California
Client
   Hunan Garden
Designer
   Bruce Yelaska

Creative Firm
Bruce Yelaska Design
(continued)

Creative Firm
The Spangler Design Team
St. Louis Park, Minnesota
Client
Mighty Wrapps
Creative Director
Marl Spangler
Designer
Laura Bartley

Creative Firm
Louis & Partners
Bath, Ohio
Client
Mr. Hero
Designer
Louis & Partners

Creative Firm
Hanson Associates, Inc.
Philadelphia, Pennsylvania
Client
Tootsies
Designer
Troy Kiick

Creative Firm
Bruce Yelaska Design
San Francisco, California
Client
Nonni's Biscotti
Designer
Bruce Yelaska

NONNI'S

Creative Firm
Designs on You!
Ashland, Kentucky
Client
Rocco's Ristorante
Designer
Suzanna M.W.

Menu of Fine Italian Wines

Welcome to Rocco's Ristorante.

I am proud to feature a variety of wines from Italy, the world's top producer of wine. Vineyards are planted in all 20 of Italy's regions, resulting in 900 million cases a year. This accounts for nearly 25% of the total world production! Italy is also earning a reputation for top quality wines, a result of changing techniques and stringent quality controls in recent years.

Wines can bring great enjoyment, but they can be confusing. Who wants to be intimidated by a bottle of wine? We've prepared this book to make wine more accessible. By learning more about Italian wines, you may choose to experiment. I'm hoping to make this even easier by doing two things: One, by lowering the prices on our bottles of wine; and two, by offering a Featured Wine of the Day available by the glass. This way, you can sample new wines without committing to a bottle until you know that you like it.

Though it's fun to learn about wines and get involved in all the terminology, I feel it's very important to remember one thing: Drink what tastes good. Enjoy!

– Rocco Muriale

Rocco's acknowledges "Hugh Johnson's Modern Encyclopedia of Wine" and "The New Frank Schoonmaker Encyclopedia of Wine" for assistance with this Wine Menu and highly recommends both books.

Rocco's

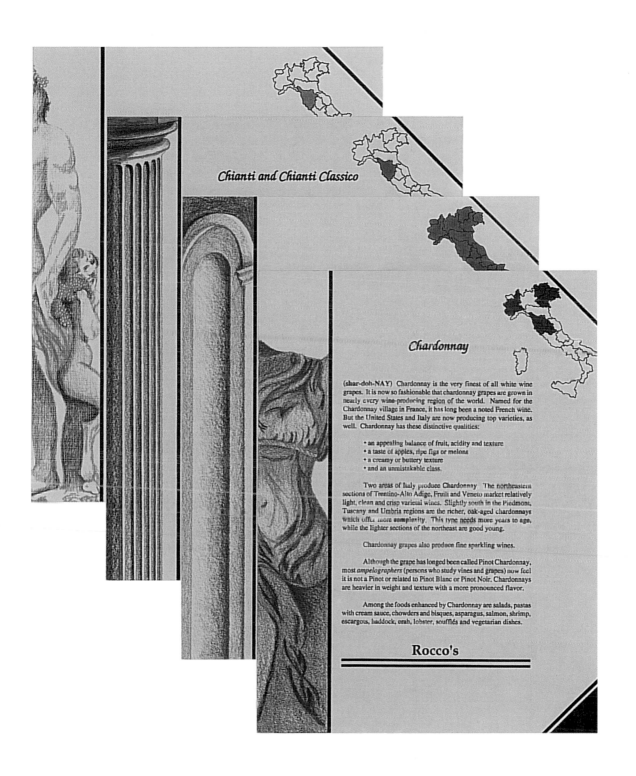

Chianti and Chianti Classico

Chardonnay

(shar-doh-NAY) Chardonnay is the very finest of all white wine grapes. It is now so fashionable that chardonnay grapes are grown in nearly every wine-producing region of the world. Named for the Chardonnay village in France, it has long been a noted French wine. But the United States and Italy are now producing top varieties, as well. Chardonnay has these distinctive qualities:

- an appealing balance of fruit, acidity and texture
- a taste of apples, ripe figs or melons
- a creamy or buttery texture
- and an unmistakable class.

Two areas of Italy produce Chardonnay. The northeastern sections of Trentino-Alto Adige, Fruili and Veneto market relatively light, clean and crisp varietal wines. Slightly south in the Piedmont, Tuscany and Umbria regions are the richer, oak-aged chardonnays which offer more complexity. This type needs more years to age, while the lighter sections of the northeast are good young.

Chardonnay grapes also produce fine sparkling wines.

Although the grape has longed been called Pinot Chardonnay, most *ampelographers* (persons who study vines and grapes) now feel it is not a Pinot or related to Pinot Blanc or Pinot Noir. Chardonnays are heavier in weight and texture with a more pronounced flavor.

Among the foods enhanced by Chardonnay are salads, pastas with cream sauce, chowders and bisques, asparagus, salmon, shrimp, escargots, haddock, crab, lobster, soufflés and vegetarian dishes.

Rocco's

Creative Firm
Di Donato Associates
Chicago, Illinois
Client
Goose Island Beer Company
Creative Director
Peter Di Donato
Designer
Don Childs

Creative Firm
Studio Hill Design
Albuquerque, New Mexico
Client
Portobello Restaurant
Designers
Sandy Hill, Emma Roberts

Creative Firm
Gray Cat Graphic Design
Chicago, Illinois
Client
The California Clipper
Designer
Lisa Empleo

Creative Firm
 CYD Design
  Milwaukee, Wisconsin
Client
 Virtual Cafe
Designer
 Cory Dewalt

Creative Firm
 KROG
  Ljubljana, Slovenia
Client
 Gostilna Pri Kuklju
Designer
 Edi Berk

Creative Firm
 Adkins/Balchunas
  Providence, Rhode Island
Client
 Sbarro Restaurant
Designers
 Jerry Balchunas, Susan DeAngelis

Creative Firm
Sayles Graphic Design
Des Moines, Iowa
Client
South Union Bakery
Designer
John Sayles

Creative Firm
Sayles Graphic Design
Des Moines, Iowa
Client
South Union Bread Cafe
Designer
John Sayles

Creative Firm
Iridium Marketing + Design/Formerly Aartvark Comm.
Ottawa, Canada
Client
Las Brisas Café
Designer
Jean-Luc Denat

Creative Firm
Georgopulos Design
Wayne, Pennsylvania
Client
Just Baked Inc.
Designer
Jonathan Georgopulos

the european eatery

Creative Firm
Alain M. Flores
Ecatepec, Mexico
Client
Knockout

Creative Firm
David Carter Design Assoc.
Dallas, Texas
Client
Atlantis Resort Casino
Paradise Island Bahamas
Designer
Tien Pham

Creative Firm
revoLUZion–Studio for Design
Neuhausen ab Eck, Germany
Client
Marcus Thiel, Backslash–Internet Bar
Designer
Bernd Luz

Creative Firm
  JGA, Inc.
    Southfield, Michigan
Client
    Players Grill–Home of the NFL Players
Designer
    Brian Eastman

Creative Firm
Pivot Design, Inc.
Chicago, Illinois
Client
Jersey Shore Subs
Designer
Brock Haldeman

Creative Firm
David Carter Design Assoc.
Dallas, Texas
Designer
Tracy Huck

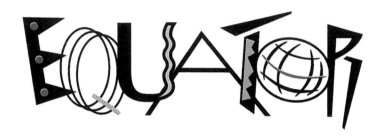

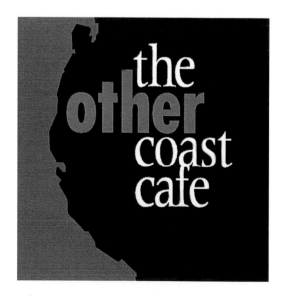

Creative Firm
Hansen Design Company
Seattle, Washington
Client
Dave Harris
Designers
Pat Hansen, Jacqueline Smith

Creative Firm
David Carter Design Assoc.
Dallas, Texas
Client
Mandalay Bay Resort & Casino
Las Vegas, NV
Designer
Tabitha Bogard

Surf Cafe

Creative Firm
David Carter Design Assoc.
Dallas, Texas
Client
Hyatt Regency Osaka
Designer
Sharon LeJeune

hit the spot

Creative Firm
Enterprise IG
London, England
Designers
Stuart Redfern, Nick Payne,
Ian McCarthy

Creative Firm
Pinkhaus Design
Miami, Florida
Client
Snapper's
Designer
Tom Sterling

Creative Firm
Hornall Anderson Design Works
Seattle, Washington
Client
Elliott's Seafood Cafe
Designers
Jack Anderson, Mary Hermes

Creative Firm
Lieber Cooper Associates
Chicago, Illinois
Client
Chart House Enterprises
Designer
Douglas K. Hardenburgh

Creative Firm
CYD Design
Milwaukee, Wisconsin
Client
Crabby Al's
Designer
Cory Dewalt

Creative Firm
O & Co.
  San Francisco, California
Client
  Scott's Restaurant
Designer
  Monica Reskala

Creative Firm
Spencer Zahn & Associates
  Philadelphia, Pennsylvania
Client
  Bookbinders
Designer
  Spencer Zahn

BOOKBINDERS
S E A F O O D   H O U S E

Creative Firm
Spencer Zahn & Associates
  Philadelphia, Pennsylvania
Client
  Bookbinders
Designer
  Spencer Zahn

Client
  Skipper's Restaurant
  Avon, Connecticut
Designer
  Todd Nickel

Creative Firm
  William Ho Design Associates Ltd.
  Hong Kong, China
Client
  Fish-Catcher Seafood Restaurant
  Phuket, Thailand
Designer
  William Ho Chung Keung

Creative Firm
  Malowany.Chiocchi.Inc.
  Boulder, Colorado
Client
  The Whale's Tail
Designer
  Gene Malowany

Scribbles Spaghetti Bar

Creative Firm
Ammirati Puris Lintas
Singapore
Client
Scribbles Spaghetti Bar
Designer
Vancelee Teng

Creative Firm
Hornall Anderson Design Works
Seattle, Washington
Client
Burgerville
Designers
John Hornall, Larry Anderson,
Bruce Branson-Meyer, Jana Nishi

Creative Firm
Addison Design Consultants Pte Ltd
Singapore
Client
International Family Food Services, Inc.
Designers
The Addison Creative Team

Creative Firm
Design Forum
Dayton, Ohio
Client
MOS Burger
Designers
The Design Forum Creative Team

Creative Firm
Lieber Cooper Associates, Sabingrafik Inc.
Chicago, Illinois
Client
Nebraska Smokehouse Co.
Art Director
Douglas Hardenburgh
Designer
Tobias Harris W.
Illustrator
Tracy Sabin

Stackwoods
Gift Certificate

The bearer of this certificate is entitled to merchandise or a selection from our menu up to the face value shown.

David P. Colon

DAVID COLON, MANAGING PARTNER STACKWOODS RESTAURANT

Creative Firm
Vrontikis Design Office
Los Angeles, California
Client
Global Dining, Inc.
Tokyo
Art Director
Petrula Vrontikis
Designer
Kim Sage

Creative Firm
Funk & Associates, Inc.
Eugene, Oregon
Client
Tres Hermanas Restaurante
Designer
Beverly Soasey

Creative Firm
Gregory group
Dallas, Texas
Client
Billy Joe's Bar-B-Que
Designer
Jon Gregory

Creative Firm
Kowalski Designworks, Inc.
Berkeley, California
Client
The Rib Line
Designer
Stephen Kowalski

Creative Firm
Monica Reskala
San Francisco, California
Client
Alegria Winery
Designer
Monica Reskala

Harvest Moon ™

The best meals under the moon.

Creative Firm
Adkins/Balchunas
Providence, Rhode Island
Client
Harvest Moon
Designers
Jerry Balchunas, Susan DeAngelis

Creative Firm
Graphic Technologies
Issaquah, Washington
Client
Remmy's Catering & Restaurant
Designer
Gary Thompson

Creative Firm
Mike Salisbury Communications
Venice, California
Client
Bouley
Designers
Mike Salisbury, Mira

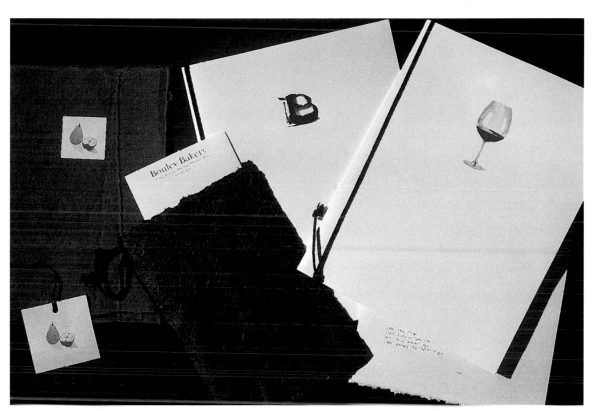

Creative Firm
Lebowitz/Gould/Design, Inc.
New York, New York
Client
Lex
Designers
Sue Gould, Amy Hufnagel

Creative Firm
Cellar Ideas
San Jose, California
Client
Mugsy's
Designer
Don Barnes

Creative Firm
Funk & Associates
Eugene, Oregon
Client
Café Yumm
Designer
Christopher Berner

Creative Firm
Bright Strategic Design
Marina Del Rey, California
Client
Hal's Bar & Grill
Designer
Keith Bright

Creative Firm
Bartels & Co., Inc
St. Louis, Missouri
Client
City Coffee House
Designer
John Postlewait

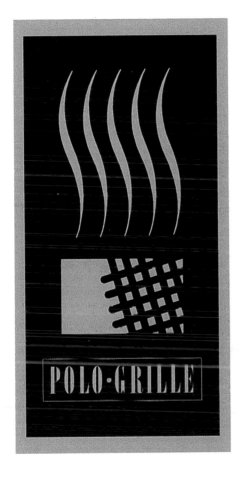

Creative Firm
Design Center
Minnetonka, Minnesota
Client
Taraccino Coffee
Design Director
John Reger
Designer
Todd Spichke

Creative Firm
Five Visual Communication & Design
West Chester, Ohio
Client
Polo Grille
Designers
Denny Fagan, Rondi Tschopp

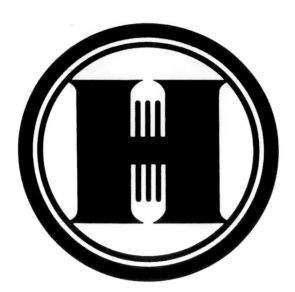

Creative Firm
EAT Advertising & Design
Kansas City, Missouri
Client
Houlihan's Restaurant Group
Designer
Paul Prato

Creative Firm
EAT Advertising & Design
Kansas City, Missouri
Client
Houlihan's Restaurant Group
Designer
Patrice Eilts-Jobe, Paul Prato

Creative Firm
Creative Vision Design Co.
Providence, Rhode Island
Client
Coffee Fields
Designer
Greg Gonsalves

Creative Firm
  Adkins/Balchunas
  Providence, Rhode Island
Client
  The Groceria
Designers
  Jerry Balchunas, Michelle Phaneuf

Creative Firm
Sayles Graphic Design
Des Moines, Iowa
Client
Racoon River Brewing Company
Designer
John Sayles

Creative Firm
Babcock, Schmid, Louis & Partners
Bath, Ohio
Client
Bob Evans

Creative Firm
Phoenix Creative, St. Louis
St. Louis, Missouri
Client
Cracker Barrel Old Country Store (30th Anniversary)
Designer
Paul Jarvis

Creative Firm
Adkins/Balchunas
Providence, Rhode Island
Client
Sbarro Restaurant
Designers
Jerry Balchunas,
Michelle Phaneuf

Creative Firm
SBG Enterprise
San Francisco, California
Client
Flagstow Corp./Advantica Restaurant Group
Designers
Mark Bergman, Richard Patterson

Creative Firm
Babcock, Schmid, Louis & Partners
Bath, Ohio
Client
Krystal

Creative Firm
Adkins/Balchunas
Providence, Rhode Island
Client
Sbarro Restaurant
Creative Director
Jerry Balchunas
Designer
Steve Rebello

Creative Firm
Sayles Graphic Design
Des Moines, Iowa
Client
Wienie Wagon
Designer
John Sayles

Creative Firm
Sibley Peteet Design
Dallas, Texas
Client
Baker Bros
Designer, Illustrator
Tom Hough

Creative Firm
Wallace Church
New York, New York
Client
Marguery Grill, NYC
Designer
Sarah Jones

Creative Firm
Signi
Mexico City, Mexico
Client
Restaurantes La Mansion
Designer
Daniel Castelao

Creative Firm
double entendre, inc.
Seattle, Washington
Client
Jackrabbit
Designers
Richard A. Smith, Daniel P. Smith
Illustrator
Michael Marshall

Creative Firm
Gardner Design
Wichita, Kansas
Client
Sergeant's
Designer
Chris Parks

Creative Firm
Gardner Design
Wichita, Kansas
Client
Big Fish
Designer
Chris Parks

Creative Firm
Trademark Design Limited
London, England
Client
The 3 Monkeys Restaurant
Designer
Clive Gay

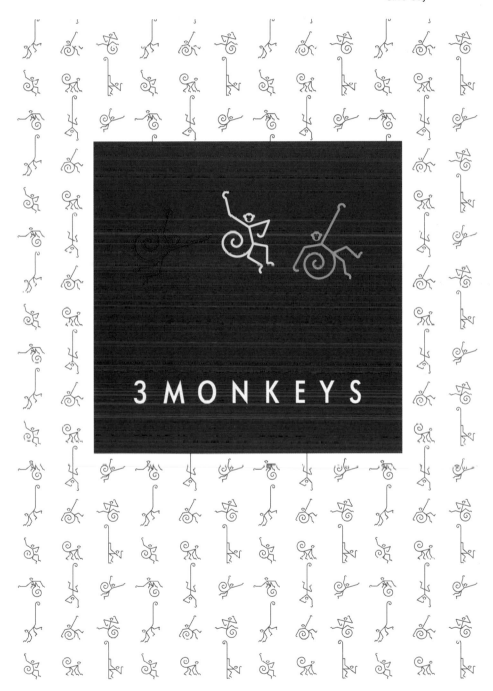

Creative Firm
CYD Design
Milaukee, Wisconsin
Client
Cafe Vecchio Mondo
Designer
Cory Dewalt

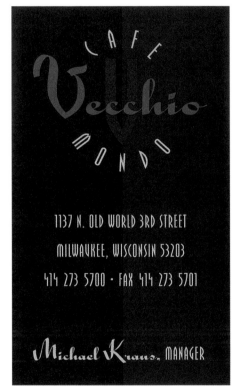

Creative Firm
Julia Tam Design
Palo Verdes, California
Client
UCLA Dining Services
Designer
Julia Tam

Creative Firm
William Ho Design Associates Ltd.
Hong Kong, China
Client
Hilltop Restaurant
Philippine
Designer
William Ho Chung Keung

Creative Firm
David Carter Design Assoc.
Dallas, Texas
Client
Hotel President Wilson
Designer
Tracy Huck

Creative Firm
Addison Design Consultants Pte Ltd
Singapore
Client
The American Club (Singapore)
Designers
The Addison Creative Team

Creative Firm
Sayles Graphic Design
Des Moines, Iowa
Client
Landmark Grille
Designer
John Sayles

Creative Firm
John Kneapler Design
New York, New York
Client
Cena
Designers
Chris Dietrich, John Kneapler

bica do sapato
restaurante esplanada cafetaria sushi bar

Creative Firm
Ricardo Mealha Atelier Design Estrate Gico
Lisbon, Portugal
Client
Bica Do Sapato Restaurant
Designer
Ana Margarida Unha

Creative Firm
Spencer Zahn & Associates
Philadelphia, Pennsylvania
Client
Winston Cafe
Designer
Spencer Zahn

Creative Firm
Spencer Zahn & Associates
Philadelphia, Pennsylvania
Client
Carlyle Grill
Designer
Spencer Zahn

Creative Firm
Cahan & Associates
San Francisco, California
Client
Jimmy Beans
Art Director
Bill Cahan
Designer
Guthrie Dolin

Creative Firm
Little & Company
Minneapolis, Minnesota
Client
D'Amico & Sons, Campiello Restaurant
Creative Director
Monica Little
Design Director
Jim Jackson
Designer
Kathy Soranno

ristorante

Creative Firm
Sayles Graphic Design
Des Moines, Iowa
Client
Basil Prosperi
Designer
John Sayles

Creative Firm
Hon Bing-wah/Kinggraphic
Hong Kong, China
Client
Elizabeth Hotel (Singapore)/Far East Organization
Designer
Hon Bing-wah

Creative Firm
Muller + Company
Kansas City, Missouri
Client
Rocco's Italian Restaurant
Creative Director
John Muller
Art Director
Mark Butsford
Designer
Brohan Watkins

Creative Firm
Kim Baer Design Associates
Venice, California
Client
Pasta Bene Restaurant
Designer
Maggie van Oppen

Creative Firm
Lieber Cooper Associates
Chicago, Illinois
Client
Piez Chicago
Designer
Doug Hardenburgh

Creative Firm
Gardner Design
  Wichita, Kansas
Client
  Hots For You
Designer
  Bill Gardner

Cafe Solé

Creative Firm
Hunt Weber Clark Associates
  San Francisco, California
Client
  Piatti Restaurant Company
Designers
  Leigh Krichbaum, Nancy Hunt-Weber

Creative Firm
Nora Shwadsky
  Mexico City, Mexico
Client
  Santa Fe Beer Factory
Designer
  Nora Shwadsky

Creative Firm
Alain M. Flores
Ecatepec, Mexico
Client
El gancho al hígado

Creative Firm
Hornall Anderson Design Works
Seattle, Washington
Client
Border Bell
Designers
Jack Anderson, David Bates

Creative Firm
Roger Christian & Co.
San Antonio, Texas
Client
Boudros
Designer
Roger Christian

Creative Firm
  Hon Bing-wah/Kinggraphic
    Hong Kong, China
Client
    Island Pacific Hotel/Sino Group
Designer
    Hon Bing-Wah

Creative Firm
Hon Bing-wah/Kinggraphic
(continued)

Creative Firm
Frank D'Astolfo Design
New York, New York
Client
Angelica Kitchen

BARLEY
HOUSE

Creative Firm
Callery & Company
Patchogue, New York
Client
Barley House
Designer
Kelley Callery

Creative Firm
Funk & Associates, Inc.
Eugene, Oregon
Client
Caffé Diva
Designer
Beverly Soasey

CAFFÈ DIVA

Creative Firm
EAT Advertising & Design
Kansas City, Missouri
Client
Kansas Beef Council
Designers
Patrice Eilts-Jobe, Paul Prato

142

ON THE TRAIL
A SUCCULENT BITE IN SIGHT

 SMOKED AND SPICED BEEF TENDERLOIN WITH CABERNET GLAZED PORTABELLA MUSHROOMS.

 TOP SIRLOIN BEEF WITH BABY GREENS, ARUGULA, GRILLED ASPARAGUS AND MANGO CHIPOTLE VINAIGRETTE

 SMOKED BEEF TENDERLOIN WITH ROASTED CORN, RIPE TOMATO RELISH AND REDSKIN MASHED POTATOES

 POT ROAST WITH CREAMY RISOTTO, ROASTED VEGETABLES AND NATURAL JUICES

 FRUIT STRUDEL WITH WHITE CHOCOLATE SAUCE

KANSAS BEEF COUNCIL

BEEF. IT'S WHAT YOU WANT.

HEN HOUSE MARKET.

Creative Firm
William Ho Design Associates Ltd.
Hong Kong, China
Client
The Bakery, Bangkok, Thailand
Designer
William Ho Chung Keung

Creative Firm
David Carter Design Assoc.
Dallas, Texas
Client
Paris Resort & Casino
Las Vegas, NV
Designer
Tien Pham

Creative Firm
David Carter Design Assoc.
Dallas, Texas
Client
Portifino Bay Hotel
Universal Studios
Orlando, FL
Designer
Emily Cain

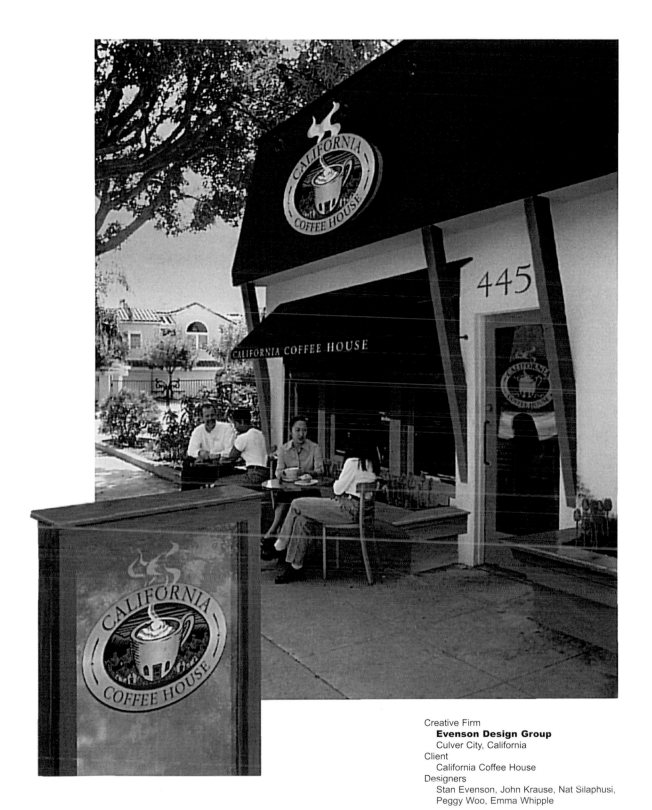

Creative Firm
Evenson Design Group
Culver City, California
Client
California Coffee House
Designers
Stan Evenson, John Krause, Nat Silaphusi,
Peggy Woo, Emma Whipple

Creative Firm
Sayles Graphic Design
Des Moines, Iowa
Client
Toscano Ristorante & Bar
Designer
John Sayles

Creative Firm
Sayles Graphic Design
(continued)

Creative Firm
Bartels & Company, Inc.
St. Louis, Missouri
Client
A Train
Designers
David Bartels, Brian Barclay

Creative Firm
Funk & Associates, Inc.
　Eugene, Oregon
Client
　Java Hut
Designer
　Beverly Soasey

Creative Firm
Simple Green Design
　Huntington Harbour, California
Client
　Cuppa Roma Coffee
Designer
　Russ Acol-Scott

Creative Firm
Via Design Inc.
　Manchester, New Hampshire
Client
　Sunburst Cafe
Designers
　Lee Perrault, George Holt

Creative Firm
Marcia Herrmann Design
Modesto, California
Client
Movin' Mocha
Designer
Marcia Herrmann

Lynda Scofield

Phone & Fax:
209-577-1517
1-800-570-1517
P.O. Box 1618
Modesto, CA 95353

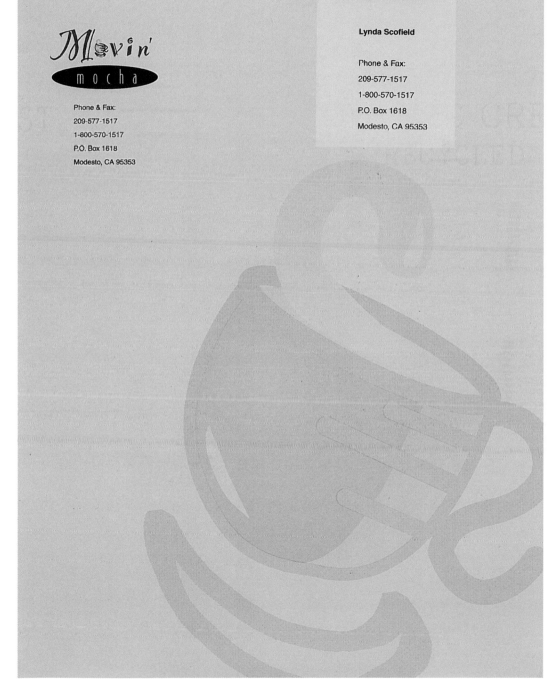

Phone & Fax:
209-577-1517
1-800-570-1517
P.O. Box 1618
Modesto, CA 95353

Creative Firm
Look
San Carlos, California
Client
Scoops Ice Cream Store
Designer
Mary Schwedhelm

Creative Firm
David Carter Design Assoc.
Dallas, Texas
Client
Mandalay Bay Resort & Casino
Las Vegas, NV
Designer
Tien Pham

Creative Firm
CYD Design
Milwaukee, Minnesota
Client
Lixx Frozen Custard
Designer
Cory Dewalt

Creative Firm
Cathey Associates, Inc.
Dallas, Texas
Client
Jwana Juice
Designer
Isabel Campos

Creative Firm
Jensen Design Associates
Long Beach, California
Client
Robek's Juice
Art Director
David Jensen
Designer
Pil Ho Lee

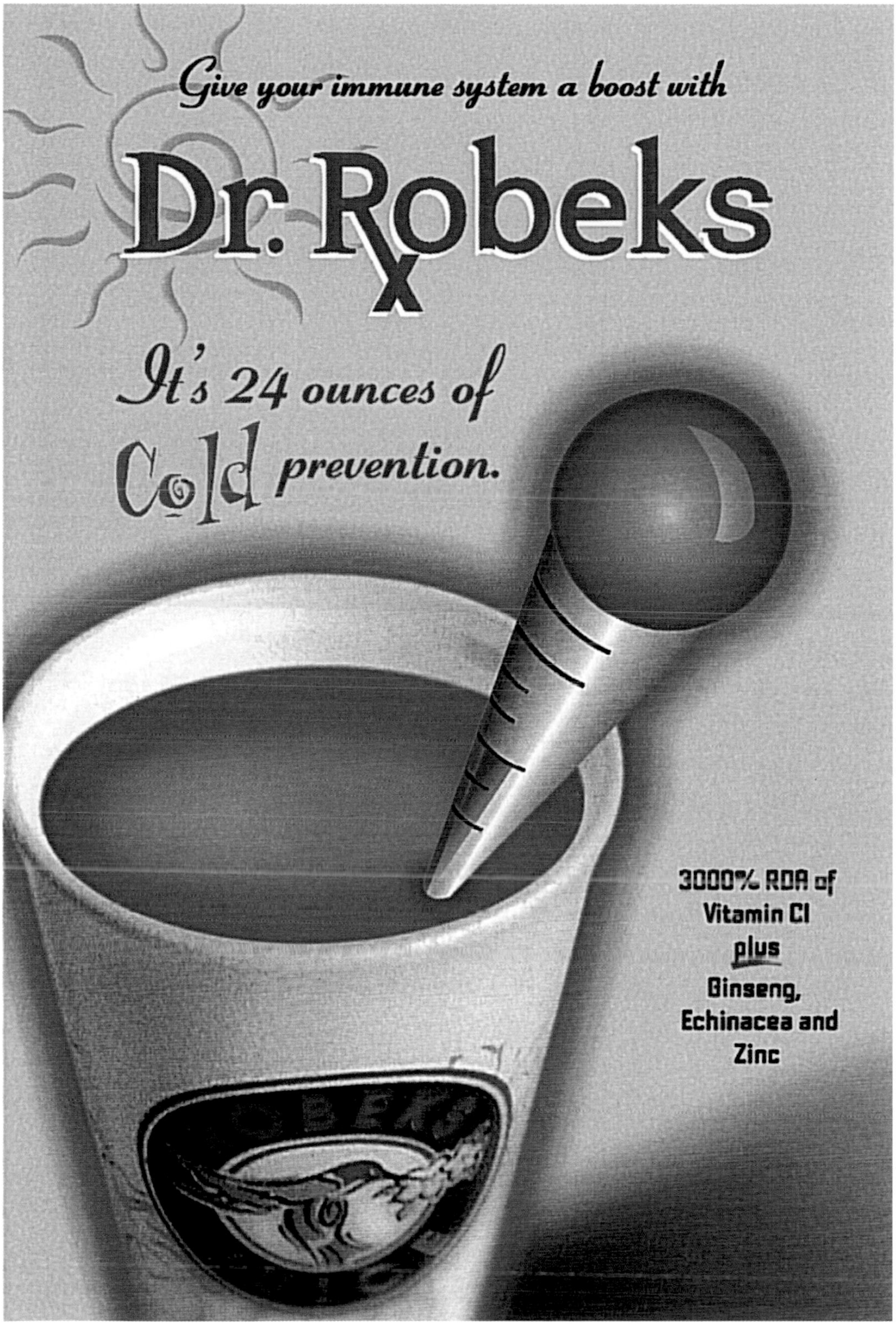
Give your immune system a boost with
Dr. Robeks
Rx
It's 24 ounces of
Cold prevention.
3000% RDA of
Vitamin C!
plus
Ginseng,
Echinacea and
Zinc

Creative Firm
Jensen Design Associates
(continued)

Creative Firm
Jensen Design Associates
(continued)

Creative Firm
Frank D'Astolfo Design
New York, New York
Client
First Stop Restaurant

Creative Firm
Frank D'Astolfo Design
New York, New York
Client
The Pink Chill

Creative Firm
Enock
New York, New York
Client
Doughnullery
Designer
David Enock

Doughnuttery

Creative Firm
  Nick Kaars & Associates
    Honolulu, Hawaii
Client
    Touch the East
Designer
    Nick Kaars

TOUCH THE EAST

Creative Firm
  Nick Kaars & Associates
    Honolulu, Hawaii
Client
  Zippy's Inc.
Designer
  Nick Kaars

Creative Firm
Rick Johnson & Co.
Albuquerque, New Mexico
Client
Gold Street Caffe
Designer
Rick Gutierrez

Creative Firm
Mires Design
San Diego, California
Client
Epicentre Teen Center
Art Director
Scott Mires
Designer
Miguel Perez
Illustrator
Tracy Sabin

FANTASTIC

FREDS

JUICE BAR

Creative Firm
Creative Vision Design Co.
Providence, Rhode Island
Client
Native, Inc.
Designer
Greg Gonsalves

Creative Firm
The Wecker Group
Monterey, California
Client
Cask One Vineyards
Designer
Robert Wecker

Creative Firm
Fuse, Inc.
Laguna Beach, California
Client
Taco Bell Nothing Ordinary About It
Designer
Russell Pierce

Creative Firm
Monica Reskala
San Francisco, California
Client
Europa Espresso Bars
Designer
Monica Reskala

Creative Firm
Robert Meyers Design
Fairlawn, Ohio
Client
Zibibbo
Designer
Robert Meyers

Creative Firm
Louey/Rubino Design Group, Inc.
Santa Monica, California
Client
Grissini
Designer
Robert Louey

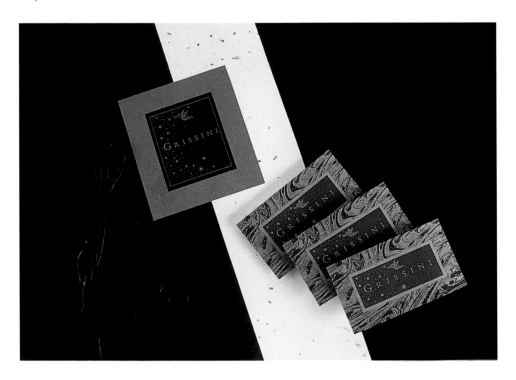

Creative Firm
David Carter Design Assoc.
Dallas, Texas
Client
Portifino Bay Hotel
Universal Studios
Orlando, FL
Designer
Emily Cain

Creative Firm
Ricardo Mealha Ateller Design
Lisbon, Portugal
Client
Lux Frágil Bar
Designer
Ana Margarida

Creative Firm
Carella + Company
North Hampton, New Hampshire
Client
Inn of Hampton/Courtyard
Designer
Linda Kirkland

Creative Firm
Ricardo Mealha, Atelier Design Estrate Gico
Lisbon, Portugal
Client
Baliza Bar
Designer
Ana Margarida Unha

Café Bar

Creative Firm
Sargent & Berman
Santa Monica, California
Client
Maple Drive Restaurant
Creative Directors
Greg Berman, Peter Sargent
Designer
Taleen Bedikian

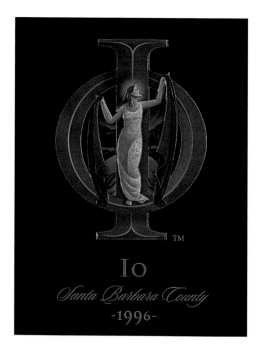

Creative Firm
Deutsch Design Works
San Francisco, California
Client
Mondavi Winery–Io Wine
Creative Director
Barry Deutsch
Designer
Dawn Janney

Creative Firm
Planet Ads & Design Pte Ltd
Singapore
Client
Ambassador Trarrit Hotel [Harilela Holding(s) Pte Ltd]
Creative Director
Harukazu Suzuki

Creative Firm
Addison Design Consultants Pte Ltd
Singapore
Client
Shihlin Electric & Engineering Corporation
Designers
The Addison Creative Team

Creative Firm
Saatchi & Saatchi Vietnam
Ho Chi Minh City, Vietnam
Client
Number 5 Bar
Saigon
Designer
Nguyen Hoa Thuan

Creative Firm
Enock
  New York, New York
Client
  Sam's
Designer
  David Enock

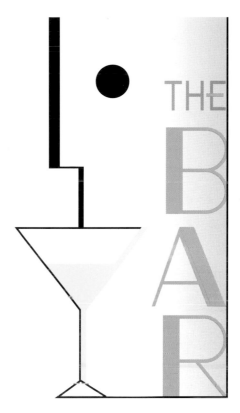

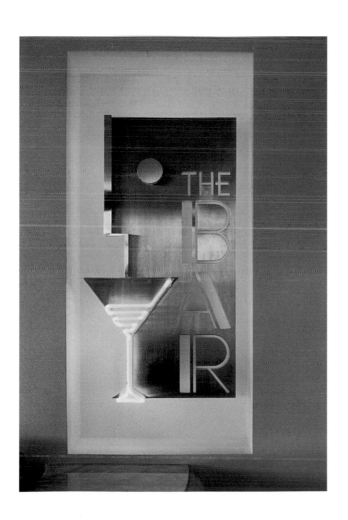

Creative Firm
Hon Bing-wah/Kinggraphic
Hong Kong, China
Client
Island Pacific Hotel/Sino Group
Designer
Hon Bing-wah

MIYAKO

Creative Firm
Dookim Inc.
 Seoul, Korea
Client
 Shilla Hotel
Designer
 Doo Kim

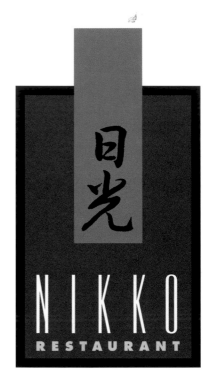

日光

NIKKO
RESTAURANT

Creative Firm
The Traver Company
 Seattle, Washington
Client
 Nikko Restaurant

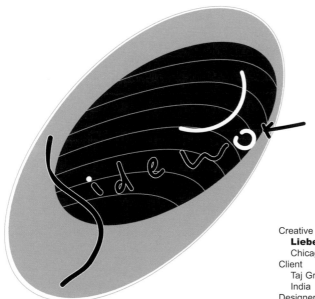

Creative Firm
Lieber Cooper Associates
 Chicago, Illinois
Client
 Taj Group of Hotels
 India
Designer
 Tobias Harris W.

Creative Firm
William Ho Design Associates Ltd.
Hong Kong, China
Client
Luhu Court Chinese Restaurant
Guangzhou, China
Designer
William Ho Chung Keung

LUHU COURT

Client
Century Harbour Hotel
Taipei, Taiwan
Designer
Chan Wing Kei, Leslie

Creative Firm
William Ho Design Associates Ltd.
Hong Kong, China
Client
Suma Japanese Cuisine
Singapore
Designer
William Ho Chung Keung

Creative Firm
Gardner Design
Wichita, Kansas
Client
Saffelli Coffee House
Designer
Travis Brown

Creative Firm
Gardner Design
Wichita, Kansas
Client
The Coffee Millers
Designer
Brian Miller

Creative Firm
Lang/Durham & Co.
Meriden, Connecticut
Client
Hastings Hotel & Conference Center
Designer
John M. Mik

110 espresso + panini bar

Creative Firm
The Traver Company
Seattle, Washington
Client
110 Espresso & Panini Bar

Creative Firm
Porter/Matjasich & Associates
Evanston, Illinois
Client
Itto Sushi Restaurant
Designer
Allen Porter

Creative Firm
Dirk Weldon Design
Miami Beach, Florida
Client
(Alex Bos) Lanna Thai Bar and Restaurant
Designer
Dirk Weldon

Creative Firm
William Ho Design Associates Ltd.
Hong Kong, China
Client
Kingston's Bar
Singapore
Designer
William Ho Chung Keung

Creative Firm
David Carter Design Assoc.
Dallas, Texas
Client
Mandalay Bay Resort & Casino
Las Vegas, NV
Designer
Sharon LeJeune

Creative Firm
David Carter Design Assoc.
Dallas, Texas
Client
Mandalay Bay Casino
Creative Director
Lori B. Wilson
Designer
Tien Pham

Client
Century Harbour Hotel
Taipei, Taiwan
Designer
Chan Wing Kei, Leslie

THE *Presidential* ROOM

Creative Firm
Addison Design Consultants Pte. Ltd.
Singapore
Client
The American Club (Singapore)
Designer
The Addison Creative Team

LOBBY LOUNGE

Client
Century Harbor Hotel
Taipei, Taiwan
Designer
Chan Wing Kei, Leslie

Creative Firm
John Kneapler Design
New York, New York
Client
Zoë
Designers
John Kneapler, Matt Waldman

Zoë

Creative Firm
 Rousso + Associates
  Atlanta, Georgia
Client
  Buckhead Life Restaurant Group
Designer
  Steve Rousso

Creative Firm
  Sayles Graphic Design
    Des Moines, Iowa
Client
  Java Joe's
Designer
  John Sayles

Creative Firm
Snodgrass Design Associates
Seattle, Washington
Client
St. Michael's Alley
Designer
Leslie Snodgrass

Creative Firm
Designs On You!
Ashland, Kentucky
Client
The Frame Up Gallery Coffee House And Tea Room
Designer
Suzanna M.W.

Creative Firm
Gable Design Group
Seattle, Washington
Client
Espresso Stop
Designers
Tony Gable, Karin Yamagiwa

Paradise Grill

Creative Firm
   EAT Advertising & Design
   Kansas City, Missouri
Client
   Paradise Grill/PB&J Restaurants
Designer
   Patrice Eilts-Jobe

Creative Firm
Simple Green Design
Huntington Harbour, California
Client
Mike & Tabi Brower
Designer
Mike Brower

Creative Firm
Di Vision Studio
New York, New York
Client
RX Restaurant Lounge At The Dylan
Designers
Christina Neri-Downey, Joanne Lew

Creative Firm
Kim Baer Design Associates
Venice, California
Client
Club Max
Designer
Ben Cziller

Creative Firm
William Ho Design Associates Ltd.
Hong Kong, China
Client
The Capital Club
Bangkok, Thailand
Designer
William Ho Chung Keung

Creative Firm
Profile Design
San Francisco, California
Client
Hotel Kinzan
Arima, Japan
Designer
Profile Design

Creative Firm
Westhouse Design
Greenville, South Carolina
Client
The Corner Pocket Food & Spirits
Designers
Jack Del Gado, Daniel Jones

Creative Firm
  Becker Design
    Milwaukee, Wisconsin
Client
    Winter Park Pub
Designer
    Neil Becker

Creative Firm
Lebowitz/Gould/Design, Inc.
New York New York
Client
Texas Texas
Designers
Sam Lebowitz, Amy Hufnagel

Creative Firm
Planet Design Company
Madison, Wisconsin
Client
Angelic Brewing Co.
Designer
Dan Lytle

Creative Firm
Little & Company
Minneapolis, Minnesota
Client
Morissey Hospitality-Pazzaluna Restaurant
Creative Director
Monica Little
Design Director
Jim Jackson
Senior Designers
Mike Lizama, Viet Do